Digging up a village

David Frankel

A book about archaeology

Digging up a village
A book about archaeology

David Frankel

For Zoe, Eloise and Guy

Melbourne
2019

ISBN 978-0-9924332-9-1

NATIONAL LIBRARY OF AUSTRALIA

A catalogue record for this book is available from the National Library of Australia

Your guides today are . . .

Archaeology is about things. And also about asking questions.

It is about people - not dinosaurs!

The Professor, who finds things and asks questions

Mrs P3674, who used to live in the village
(we don't know her real name, but you could give her a nicer one)

4

Everyone uses things all the time.

Archaeologists use them to find out what people did in the past
                    – or even what we do now.

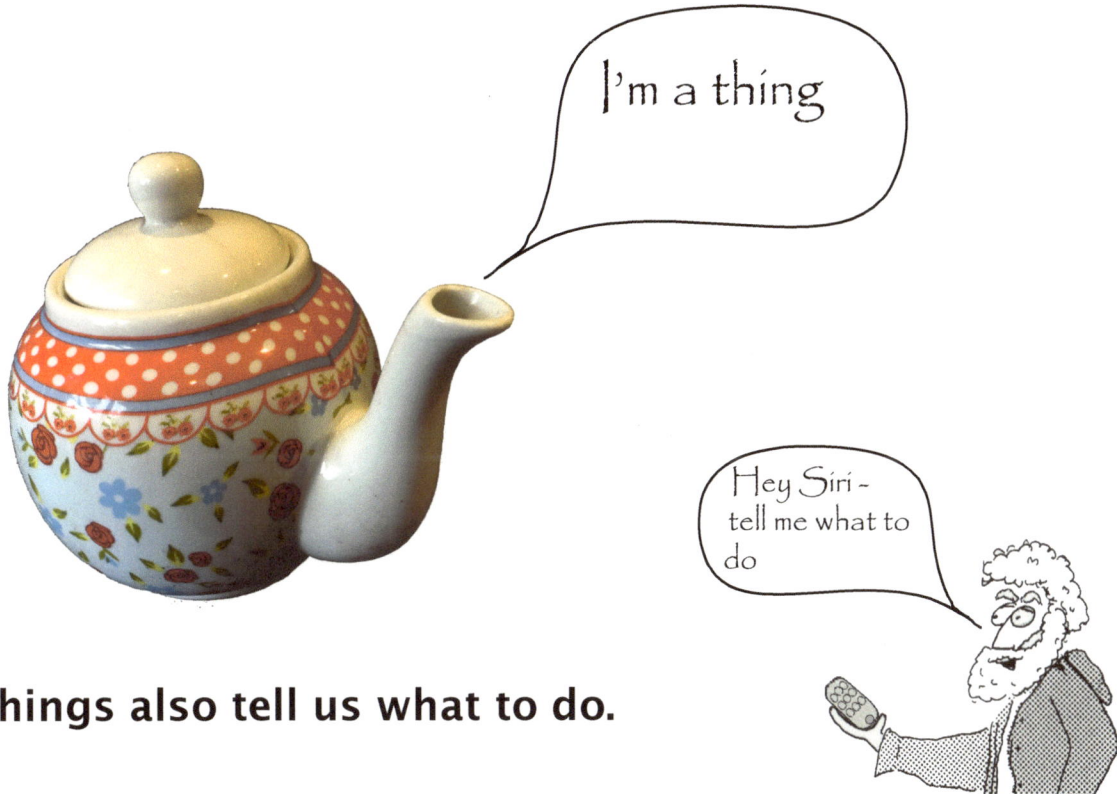

I'm a thing

Hey Siri – tell me what to do

Things also tell us what to do.

Sometimes we know what things are for . . .

I'm a little teapot

. . . and sometimes we don't.

what am I ?

6

People use things all the time . . .

would you like a cup of tea?

sometimes they break them . . .

Ooops!

7

and sometimes lose them or ...

where's my phone?

can you find my peeler?

8

. . . throw them away or leave them behind in old houses before they fall down.

I'm falling to pieces !

I'm ruined !

4,000 years ago there was a village here in Cyprus.

Now there isn't much to see – except goats.

But . . .

... bits and pieces in the ploughed soil tell us that people once lived there.

Tom, Sharon and their friends start digging.

There's so much earth to move.

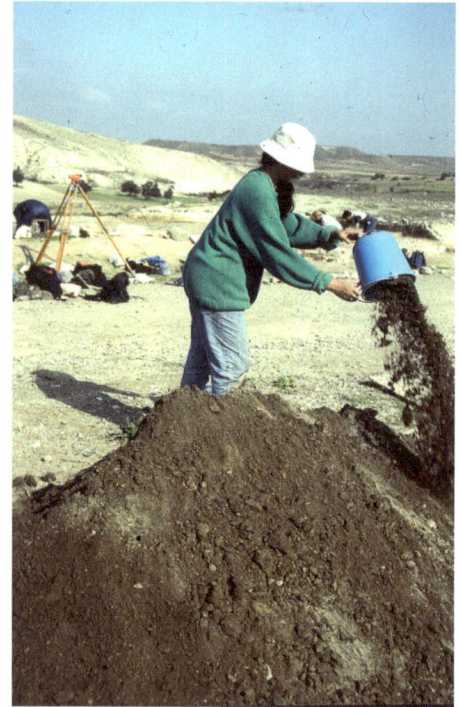

Soon the stones of old walls begin to appear just below the surface.

And then we can dig deeper inside
the remaining walls.

it's still hard work

Everyone is very busy as they dig deeper down.

How many things are they doing?

Cleaning the floor of one very neat house.

I left it very tidy!

Let's look at it properly on the next page

We've dug all the earth out of the house.

I'm so proud of my beautiful house

hearth and hob

setting for storage jar

plaster bench

hearth

post to hold up the roof

oven

bin

settings for large storage jars

low work bench

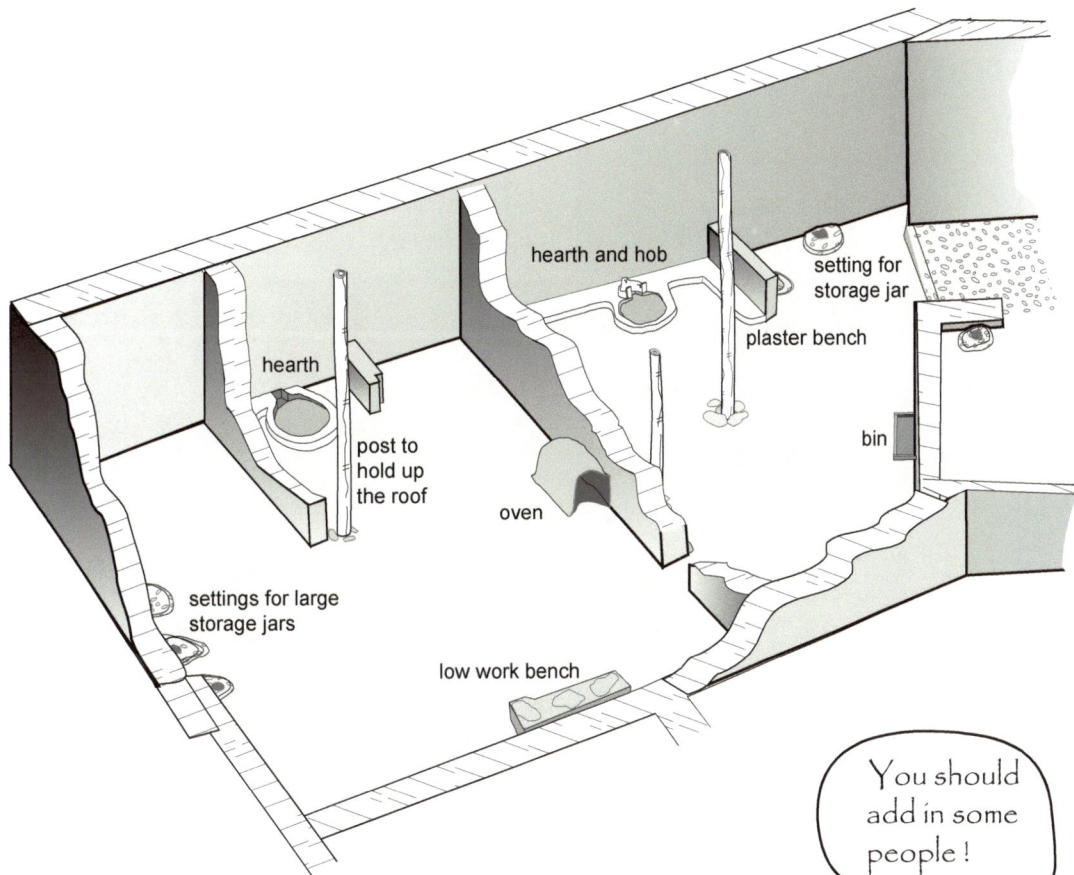

You should add in some people!

There are many built in features: low benches, fireplaces, an oven and some solid settings where large pottery storage jars were fixed in place.

People must have knelt, squatted or crouched down much of the time.

17

Dorella is cleaning a low plaster bench, bin and fireplace in this room. You can see the door just above her back.

When the family who lived there decided to move out they took all their things with them.

But they forgot something! Can you see it?

I hope they weren't too upset later on.

Where is my favourite little pot? How will I feed my little baby?

I think it had fallen off the bench and when the owner looked to see if there was anything left as she went out the door it was out of sight

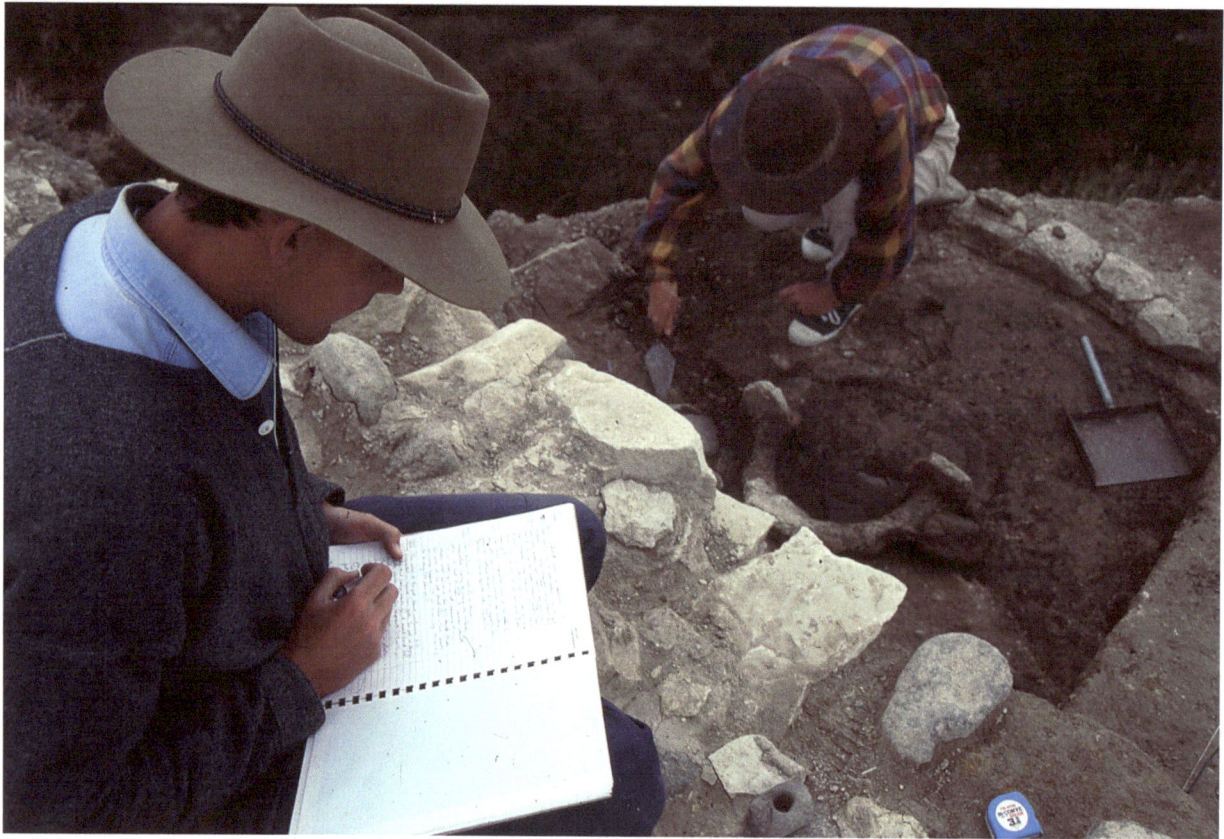

Peter is writing notes about what he and Julia have found next to a wall. It is a fireplace and pot-stand used for cooking.

When they took away the fireplace and dug deeper, they found an older wall which had been demolished before the upper one was built in its place.

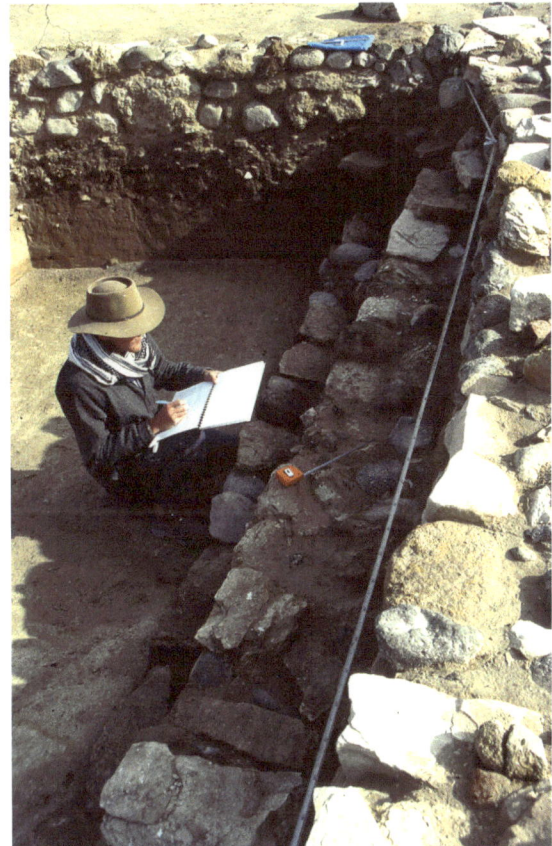

Digging deeper still they found a third, even earlier, wall from an older building.

Delese is busy drawing a plan of a fireplace in front of a bench. There is a low wall around it – maybe to stop the baby crawling into the fire.

Delese's plan shows the walls and the fire-place

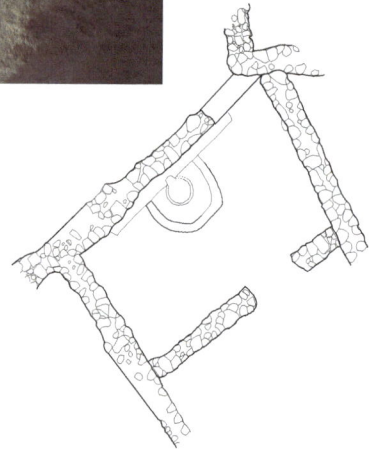

Delese's bench and fireplace were built along the wall on the left of the small room. The door is in the wall on the right.

There is a story of changes in this room. But you have to look carefully at the floor and at the wall behind the bench. I'll explain on the next page.

This part of the wall is built of bricks, not stones. There was once a door here before the bench and fireplace were built in front of it

Can you see the white outline of an older fireplace and bench just poking through the floor in front of the doorway?

Some time earlier the wall on the right was complete, with a fireplace and bench in front of it. Later these were covered by a new floor and a door made in the wall.

These two plans show the room at different times.

Earlier   **Later**

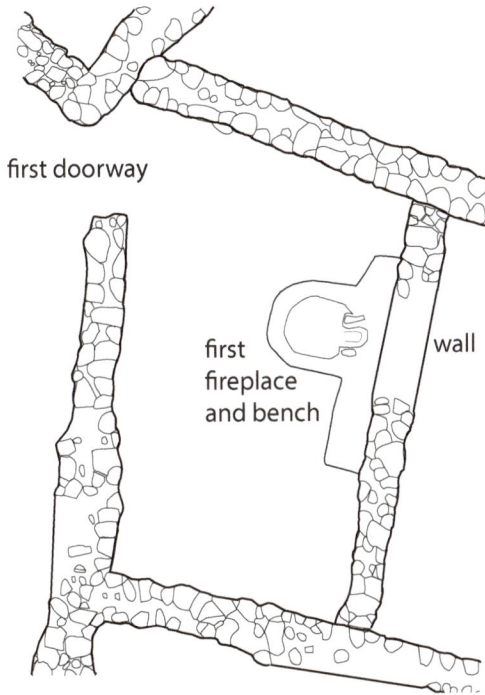

first doorway

first fireplace and bench

wall

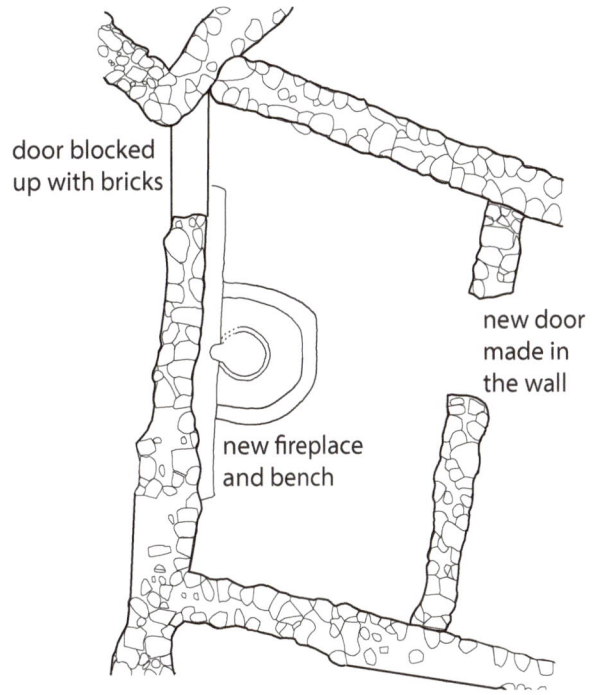

door blocked up with bricks

new door made in the wall

new fireplace and bench

The builders did a good job of my renovations

the plans show the changes in this space.

Looking at the way all the houses were built, renovated or fell into ruins we can see how the village changed over 400 years.

2,300 BCE

2,100 BCE

26

2,000 BCE

1,900 BCE

400 years is a very long time

You can keep goats in the ruins

What has Jacinta found?

It's my old cooking pot

People in the village had small fireplaces and put the cooking pots on hobs or stands like those found by Peter, Julia and Delese. Sometimes these were decorated.

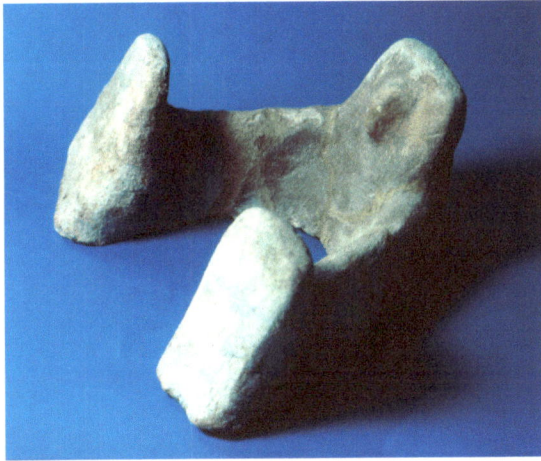

29

Cooking pots come in different sizes - big family or party-size, middle size and small sizes.

Perhaps they cooked stew
- or maybe soup
- or perhaps porridge.

just like the 3 bears

Why do these pots have one handle bigger than the other?

They could have washed up after themselves!

There were hundreds of animal bones. Paul could tell that they mainly the bones of sheep, goats and cattle. But there were also some donkeys and dogs.

Cattle were used to pull ploughs

Donkeys could carry loads

31

People grew wheat and barley, chickpeas and lentils, figs and olives and almonds and pistachio. Robyn and Dianne found the tiny remains of these plants.

Wheat and barley were ground into flour using heavy grindstones.

32

As well as cooking in pots and pans, people baked food in small ovens like this one.

We know most of the ingredients, but not the recipes

This grind-stone is really very heavy!

People had to make their own thread and cloth.

These whorls helped the spindle spin fast to draw out and twist wool.

Ephrosini shows us how a spindle is used

Weights were attached to threads on a loom to keep them taught when weaving cloth

Copper was used for tools and ornaments.

knife   razor   dress pin   earring

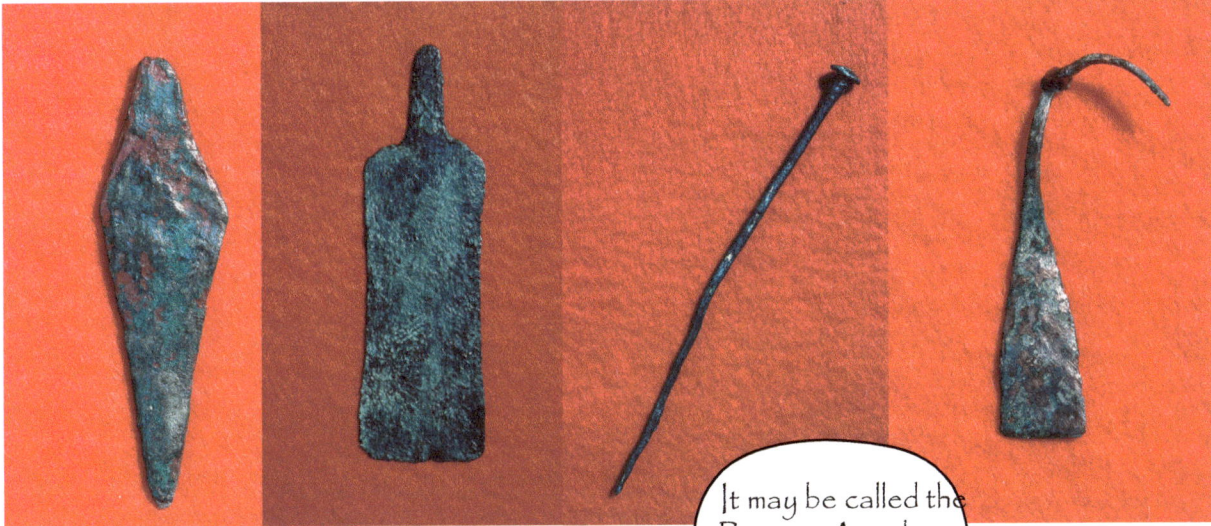

It may be called the Bronze Age, but mostly people used copper

Bronze has a bit of tin added to copper.

Stone moulds for casting copper.

35

What has Jacinta found now?

It's a beautiful stone disc. What could it be used for?

These very small ornaments would have been hung on necklaces

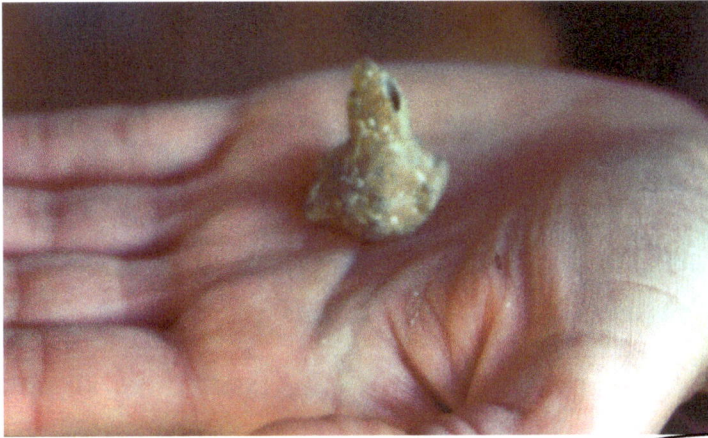

This tiny pot is only as big as your thumb.
Was it a toy?

Can you tell that these little clay things are bulls?
Were they also toys?

37

Things like this were roughly made of stone.

Some have a spiral of little hollows chipped on the top, others have 3 rows of nine hollows.

What do you think they are?

I think that these were for board games. We don't know the rules, but you could make some up

38

We found just *so much* pottery. It was used for storing, cooking and eating.

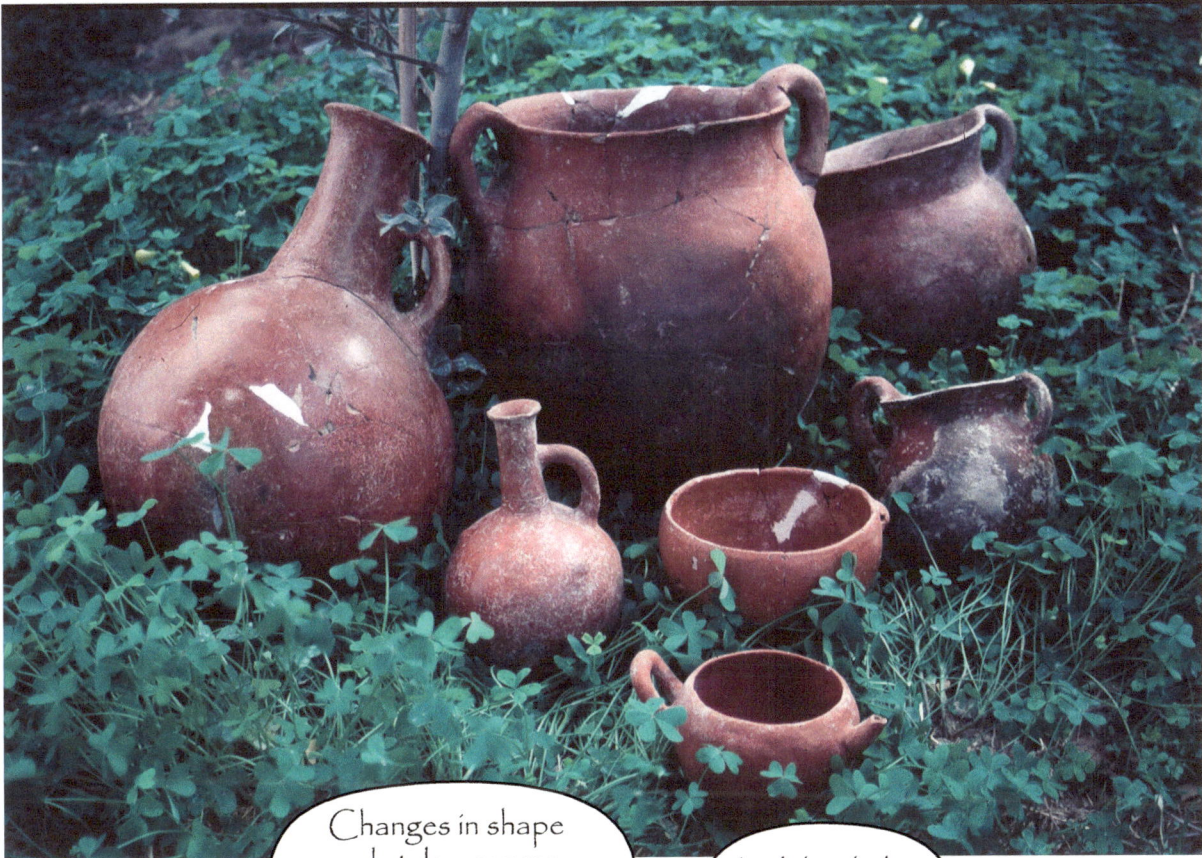

Changes in shape and style mean we can work out which are the oldest and the newest types

And that helps us tell how old the houses are

A few pots were not broken, but most were smashed to pieces.
So, we found hundreds and thousands of small fragments.

Of course they all needed to be scrubbed clean!

We collected 313,325 pieces.
How many pots were broken?

Such clumsy people!

Who is good at sums?

The village was used for about 400 years
313,325 ÷ 400 = 783 fragments of pottery for each year

How many pieces make up 1 broken pot?
Perhaps about 30, do you think?
783 ÷ 30 = 26 pots broken each year

If there were 10 families, then that means only 2 or 3 pots were broken by each family each year

Maybe not so clumsy after all!

Tim's special super-power
is finding pieces that
come from the same pot
and then sticking them
back together.

He needs a lot
of glue

42

Tim's used white plaster to fill in where pieces are missing

43

While most people were digging up all those things, others were kept very busy sorting, counting, measuring, describing, photographing and drawing them – once they had been washed and sometimes mended.

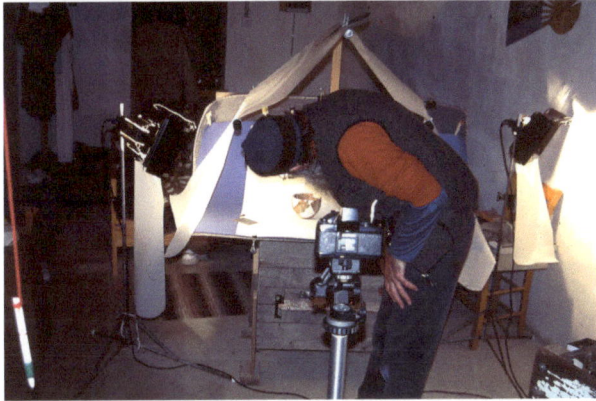

Jenny, Penny, Rudy and Greg are hard at work

45

Finally . . .

All the bits and pieces we found were safely packed away in the Cyprus Museum storerooms.

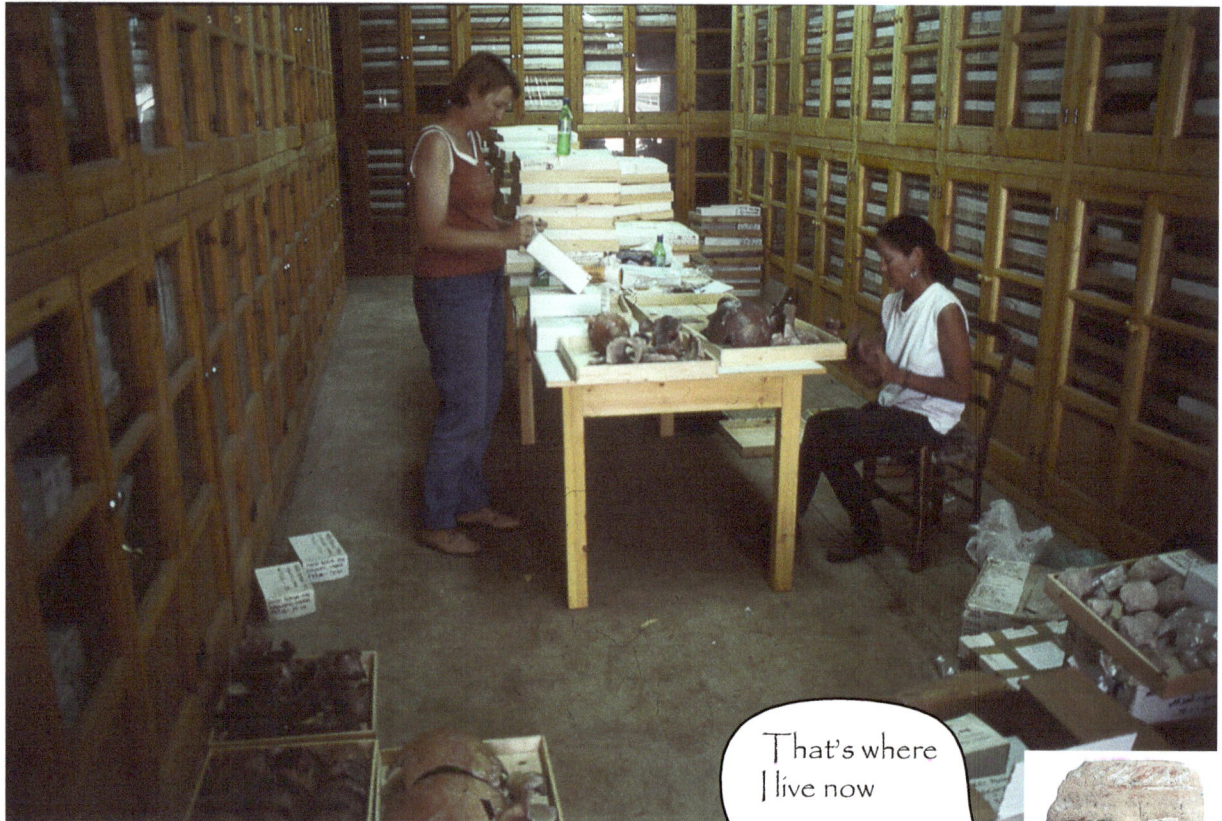

That's where I live now

But there is still something left to do !

And that is to put all the information together so that other archaeologists know what we found.

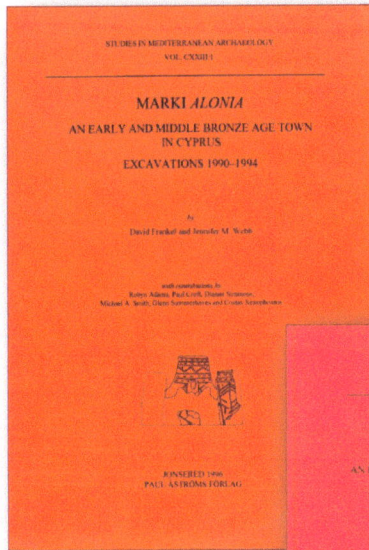

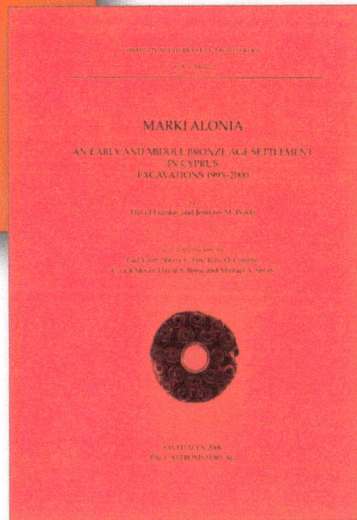

And that is the end of the story !

47

But. . . *not quite.* There are always more questions to ask and more things to find and to find out.

What were their names?

Where were the toilets?

What were their beds like?

Did they ever eat snails or frogs?

Did they brush their teeth?

What colour shoes did they wear?

Was everyone happy?

I don't know

I don't know

I don't know

I don't know

I don't know

I don't know

I don't know

Do you mind me asking all these questions?

Of course not. If you don't ask me, you won't find out anything

The excavations at Marki were carried out under a permit from the Department of Antiquities, Cyprus. I would like to thank all those in Cyprus who welcomed us and helped make the excavations possible.

Funding for the fieldwork was provided by the Australian Research Council. This was more than matched by the contributions of the very many students who travelled to Cyprus to help. This book gives a glimpse of just how much hard work they did. Artefact photos were taken by Rudy Frank.

The idea for this book was developed after Zoe arranged for me to give a talk to her classmates at Mont Albert Primary School. Lena encouraged me to write it just as she has supported all my other endeavours.

Permission to publish these four images has been kindly provided by the Department of Antiquities, Cyprus:
p. 6. Multiple vessel from Vounous
p. 19. Clay figurine of a woman holding a baby from Lapithos
p. 31. Model ploughing scene from Vounous
p. 32. Clay figures of women at work

The drawing of 'The Professor' is based on one by my friend Mike Pickering which appeared in the journal *Antiquity* 68 (1994).

REPUBLIC OF CYPRUS

File No. 42/90
Tel. 357(2) 865888
Fax. 357(2) 303148

MINISTRY OF COMMUNICATIONS AND WORKS
DEPARTMENT OF ANTIQUITIES
NICOSIA

THE ANTIQUITIES LAW CAP. 31
AND LAW 48 OF 1964 SECTIONS 14 AND 16
LICENCE TO EXCAVATE

KNOW ALL MEN BY THESE PRESENTS that I, Sophocles Hadjisavvas, Director of the Department of Antiquities, Cyprus (hereinafter called "the Director") by virtue of the powers vested in me by section 14 of the Antiquities Law (Cap. 31) and Law 48 of 1964 have granted and hereby grant to **Dr David Frankel and Jenny Webb, of La Trode University Bundoora, Victoria, Australia** (hereinafter called the "lincensee"), this licence to carry out scientific excavations with the object of discovering antiquities, subject to the provisions of section 16 of the said Law (Cap. 31 and Law 48 of 1964) and subject to the following terms and conditions:

1. The excavations may be carried out by the Licensee at **Alonia** in the village **Marki**, Nicosia District.

Thank you everyone!

49

David Frankel and Jenny Webb directed the Australian research at Marki all through the 1990s. It is the most extensive excavated area of a settlement of the Early and Middle Bronze Age in Cyprus, with a long history of occupation between about 2300 to 1900 BCE.

If you want to know more, the most convenient general introduction is:

David Frankel and Jennifer M. Webb, 2008. *Marki. Life in a Cypriot Bronze Age Village*. Moufflon Publications, Nicosia.

There are also many specialist studies on the site and its significance. For those who want to explore further, these two are a good place to start:

David Frankel and Jennifer M. Webb, 2006. Neighbours. Negotiating space in a prehistoric village. *Antiquity* Volume 80, pages 287-302.

David Frankel and Jennifer M. Webb, 2012. Household continuity and transformation in a prehistoric Cypriot village. Pages 473-500 in B.J. Parker and C.P. Foster (editors), *New Perspectives on Household Archaeology*. Eisenbrauns, Winona Lake.

If you are really, really serious, these two big red books report the results of the excavations in detail:

David Frankel and Jennifer M. Webb, 1996. *Marki Alonia. An Early and Middle Bronze Age Town in Cyprus. Excavations 1990-1994*. Studies in Mediterranean Archaeology CXXIII:1, Jonsered.

David Frankel and Jennifer M. Webb, 2006. *Marki Alonia. An Early and Middle Bronze Age Settlement in Cyprus. Excavations 1995-2000*. Studies in Mediterranean Archaeology CXXIII:2, Sävedalen.

www.ingramcontent.com/pod-product-compliance
Lightning Source LLC
Chambersburg PA
CBHW042010090426
42811CB00015B/1606